With Life, Of Love, & On Dying

I0162938

Copyright © 2021 Columbus M. Richard.

All rights reserved. This book or any portion thereof may
not be reproduced or used in any manner whatsoever
without the express written permission of the publisher
except for the use of brief quotations in a book review.

ISBN: 978-1-7358608-0-0 (Paperback)
ISBN: 978-1-7358608-1-7 (Hardcover)

Front cover image by S. Richard.
Book design by Columbus M. Richard.
Richard Media & Publications, LLC

With Life, of Love, & On Dying by Columbus M. Richard

With Life, Of Love, & On Dying

WITH LIFE

A collection of assorted poems, tributes, and eulogies for
the lives lost and remembered...
In writing them have found the key to this non-existent
truth that man calls happiness
The moment shadowed by tranquility and peace
The world laughs, yet I weep; with nothing and no one
Lonely
This existence brings darkness
From what once gave me joy in the music
Everchanging
This monstrosity rings
Loudly, and deafening
Enticing I find the quiet, in emptiness I am lost
I find myself again in my solitude, with my sounds.
Lonely, enticing, and loud.

I listen to visualize the heart of the human mind
Broken as shards of glass, lost by moonlight; crescent and
full
As I once was
But her light seems to no longer burn for me
Again finding comfort in the bittersweet melodies
Hymns of nothingness, or about the love that won't exist

I find truth, not in the words of others, or even myself
But simply, in knowing
Life seems to be distant
To be alive, and searching
Eternally

Yet we seem to measure it by how loud the cries of our
children are ignored

I see space. Not outer, the inner.
Of it all. All of the known features and faces
Of what seems to exist.
We call out to be heard but gain nothing.
Other than sight, slighted
Blurred and forever distorted
Adjusted by man

I know pain
Countless attacks made towards and against the womb
The whole
Man
Leaving creation to be abandoned
Equated with destruction
Desecrating our mothers to make the male all-powerful
So much so that the gods we serve have become like man,
the male King

The Remnant

"Children have not changed," she says.
Well does she not know of our youth?
how our babies are killing each other
of their deaths at the hands of mothers, burning and
broken since the womb?
or forgotten, locked in bondage.
well maybe the children have not changed,
but the world will never be the same.
between protecting our own,
by locking them up and even raiding their homes.
to constantly ill-educating them with nonsense
filled with lies coded in a glimpse of history.
a system based on red-boned blue-eyed mists of the past
slavery reminiscent times,
that has been excused by seemingly gotten equality still
shadowed by inferiority.
yet we still give our youth years and years,
of useless bullshit called knowledge
to then only to deny them a white sheet of paper.
instead making them a statistic
of an over-sexed crazed race of men
caged, fertile and grave bidden.
the women
emotionally, both lost and broken harshly
repopulating the world with…
the Children
who grow wounded and abandoned?

she says, "The children have not changed."
does she remember those who lose their mothers to HIV,
drugs, violence, and giving life?

hopeless, inescapable
or those growing up with no father
searching for manhood alone
lost in the bedroom, strip clubs, or tied down by lies told
by other men

she says that "The children are the Remnant"
"those set apart, by God Himself"
a chosen few
along with "God never gives us more than we can bear"
but we have carried so much that we ourselves have
become barren

she speaks of wisdom mixed with old age and mercy
we speak of the tales and experience of NOW!
of the experiences and hardships that left us shaken
is this to be what we call life?
or is it, how they say, "what you make it."
maybe this is a song left on repeat
forgotten by ancestors
of a distant yesterday
but is this echo so loud
that we cannot ignore it
that it cannot be let go
is this all we all we are to know
as the ummm… The Remnant
Are we truly set apart?
I expect it to be different
but the tears have stained our eyes so much that it bleeds
what are we to do in a disaster?
predestined since the beginning
is this something we embrace?

With Life, Of Love, & On Dying

and she says the children have not changed…

What Needs to Be Said (March 13, 2006)
Your face disappeared and your presence is no longer
here
I sought after you but instead I found your heart
It seems in your absence that we are no longer apart
I looked and saw your face in the clouds the other day
The memory of your memories helped ease the pain and
made time slip away

Your voice no longer heard
With no need for a last word
I hear you though, whistling in the trees
Floating through the breeze
Now I know you are free
The sound of weeping is all I hear
But even in the silence I know there is no fear
 So, listen from the east to the west
 Sounds of an angel no longer in flesh

Your warm loving embrace is gone
But your spirit resides in its place
I feel you in everything I do and be
Is that how it is meant?
I live for you, you stay alive through me?
Your touch, yes, your touch, we long for
You're in all us and will be forevermore
Maybe I will know with every grip to hold tighter
Longer, maybe
To feel love and satisfy my soul's hunger

Now look at me, looking for you
But me, in me, it is me. I am you.

With Life, Of Love, & On Dying

You flow in and out, through and through
Forever in me that is what holds true
Your place, cannot nobody fill
We remember you, and we always will
Need you, want you, hurt for you,
You make it better, even now you still do
The pain, these feelings, and thoughts flowing in and out
of my head
So, remember us, we remember you and your life.
We love you until, there is forever.
and that is all that needs to be said!

My Pain (May 28, 2006)

Only me, yet I do not show it
Myself that is
I must not know it
Seen as by you
Well, this life is not true
Lies, lies, lies tie me to this spot
Trying and trying as my soul rots
This is not right at all for me
What am I? What have I come to be?
A dream, an illusion, or some sort of deceit.
brought upon constantly by self-defeat.
This life, this time, this way is not right
To be and to be would be all worth the fight
What shall, what can, what will I do?
Again, and again until I am finally through
To show then prove, and be set on the side
Where will I go from whence, I cannot hide?
In the front or on the top
Do you see me now?
I can but did not, have not I made you proud
Over and over, I have become what you say
My life, now yours, can it be no other way
Is it if I feel bad you feel?
You hurt me and you
I always knew that you would
You have ruined it all and taken my soul
Freed from this life is my one true goal
All I want from this life for the sake of my name
Is to escape from this shame and feel no paid…

I Want Me (April 23,2006)

Every day I look for and think if I am a son, and I try and
try to find someone
Someone, who can be, satisfies my need, and helps me to
be free
Free to be him, that man, searching to find him and
knowing he could not be him
Them, the ones who have held and was shared a moment
and only left because
Because I wanted and knew the meaning, my life, and my
story they could no longer be in.

Once before I knew why, of how men cried, becoming
entangled in a meaning in nothing but a lie
A lie told once before by the others, telling him that he
was not and could never be one of the brothers
A brother with stability, the skills, and all that stuff; but
still never was he allowed to be rough
Rough in the game, he only did the same, which was to
stay by himself learning to love only in names
His name was said, said to be all in his head, changed
over and over by the ones that wanted him dead

I have found the way, despite being left in the darkness
for the better parts for all day
So, there I stayed looking for my heart seeking to find
where it was that I was torn apart.
Torn apart by the thought of myself, loving who I thought
I was proved bad for my health
There I grew sick and lost half my mind, but I saw what it
was; what I was hoping to find

So, I know what had been set apart for me, all I ever
wanted was what I was that I need
All I want is, I want me

Death of A Lady (May 22, 2007)

(The Death) 3/3/2007
Around eleven/midnight… Drop
My spirit floats
floating
As though I am lost
Yet it feels so
I do not know
A bit of happiness mixed with
AHHHH…
She is no more
I weep
Long hard deadly tears
But why
I have longed for this moment
And in all
It
  Is
    All!!
This grandeur of a moment
comes at the climax
of my teaching.
Funny (Hah!)
I lose my heart
when I grow
Ain't that something?
She is no more
I bear it alone
My hope
my mind
my life
It is…

(She is No Moore) 5/22/2007
Among my class
Alone among at least 100+
No one MATTERS
I search for her face
But it is not.
In the midst I see no shadow, nothing
No apparition
She is No Moore.

Stream of Conscious (July 23, 2010)

I AM.
I am writing.
They are watching.
I am writing that they are watching.
What am I writing while they watch?
Meaningless words.
I am thinking.
I am trying to think what they are thinking
But still they are watching.
I continue to write.
As long as they watch I shall write.
But what? Writer's block.
Writer, block those that watch as you write what you
think.
So I write.
I will continue to write.
I am a writer.
I have been writer.
Write, right.

Again
I am writing.
Again, just writing.
I am still sitting and thinking.
Yet again.
Now what am I thinking?
I am thinking "what will I write?"
I see what I am thinking
On paper I write what I think that I see
They are listening
They are trying to hear what I am writing

But did they not see it?
How can they hear the words that write?
Watch me write.
Listen to the words that I write
It is alright
For we must write, for life
write for it is right.

I continue
I am continuing to live and write.
They laugh
Now they are laughing
Do they laugh because I write?
Or because I write that they are laughing
They will not stop
So I will not stop
Writing, that is.
I cannot stop writing, and so
I do not listen
I just write that they laugh even though I do not listen to
them laugh while I write.
I should write of love
Or should I love what I write?
Or simply write LOVE?
But how do I write, love?
Is it Eros?
Is it phileo?
Agape?
I write all three.
God is.

I write God is LOVE.

Surely God loves me
So I shall continue to write of God
I shall continue to write God loves.
Write love.
Write.

Fuck It, Write (July 23, 2010)

I write to create, but my creations will not obey me
outside of these lines.
They see the creator abandoned.
So they rebel
In it
Outside of these lines they take corporal
Form, freely and knowingly they give chase to my rebuke
Running madly and angrily
Seeking to destroy my deepest secrets and ambitions
Left away
Because

I write to be free, but my words provide no form of
escape.
The adventure once found in writing no longer my own
No means of transportation can be found
No vehicular or automotive in ink
Just this sinking ignorance
Pulling me away from my mind, enchanting my words
For another
Until again I write
Of nothing, but of how I long to get away
With you.

I write my name and yours
You lover, who are you
I see you as you are and as mine
But you see nothing unless you see bills
Encoded with a myth tracing "In God We Trust"
But my lover why I write for you
I do not know

With Life, Of Love, & On Dying

I still write for you because I love you as you can created
and become
I long for you because in error I have hurt you
Deeply and unknowing
I continue writing you beautiful name
SO much so that your name has crept into my household
and kinsman
The memory of your name spoken every time I see her
Bearing your name
So, will I ever write of how we loved…?

each other

I write to smile, but in writing I have no face, value.
No illustration can detail the words I write in front of my
face
Once again, I can run
Madly and fiercely on the wings of this paper.
Until my words end, and end.
I write.
Maybe if he were written as my lover on paper, he would
have to love me.
Lest I write of my end, will it become "The End"
If I gave up writing, then would I value what I face?
But still of these things I alone know nothing.
Fuck it, Write.

OF LOVE

Of the many things I know and have known of love
One thing is certain
The potential in a future
Seems so distant…
Beautiful… surreal. Yet Frightening.
Inevitable assumptions cloud my judgement
And get the best of me
Leaving way to doubt and mistrust
because of another…

Love kknows no age
Not tolerance
Just regret, shame, and a bitter longing
For escape from loneliness is the main goal
Yet this goal keeps us entranced
Entrapped
By that which we fear the most
This dark side of love
Loneliness, the yearning
Bitterness and envy

War of the Minds

I remember wanting to know what love is
Not Hollywood's version where ol dude fucks ol girl, gets
her pregnant, marries, then divorce.
That is tired!!!

Remember fasting from fake and selfish people
When I no longer ate at the food of the table of my earthly
family

I remember wanting to have arms to run to
To be met with a warm embrace
and a shoulder to cry on...

This Love is My Weakness (June 21, 2008)

You do know I'm a boy, right?...
Words spoken with only a glance
Loudly, profound even more than true sound
While questioning whether it was even true
Truth found in life being "true-ly" worth living
Regardless
Having observed and known all ills and struggles
Similar to those seeming to exist
So for me
I become an island on a faraway coast
Far away even from my own clutches
Somewhat like the most precious of jewels
Formed by two and belonging to none
Wishing to be wanted, needed even by all
Still lost in a new world
Do they yearn for me?
Or will they continue to shy away?
And repeatedly take away my heart?
Continuously dragging it into deeper shit
All because I ceased to be just easy
And wanted to be just a little closer
Sometimes I called just for your tone
But that only made me seem clingy

You may try to love me
But you always lose sight
of who I am
Every,
Single
Time.
Even when you bring me down

With Life, Of Love, & On Dying

And go in for the kill
This love is my weakness
and I hate what it brings

I love you like you were mine and my own
But I steal from your heart
Living on your sadness
I fear how you feel
I give you an ear and a false sense of joy
Locking you down shattering your soul
Cause quite frankly
I love more when you are hurting
I get your presence more often
Then you cry and cry
Don't you need me to live?
Cause when I say I got you
you love how it feels
Because I could never be lonely
Just maybe you should
Cause our love is a weakness
But my heart still beats for our love.

Letter to Myself (March 13, 2008)

Do you know what I want?
Of course, you do…
Cause what I want, you want
What is it then, that we want?
Seems I forgot,
while hoping to give what others see.
Mainly them claiming this person is me.

Minus a little confidence
Just enough maybe, to let them hear me sing
Open my voice
Like I do in my heart, shower, or when I am alone.
With a sprinkle of self-worth too
Cause I always say how I feel
Letdowns, lies, and broken vows
When will they end?
The flaws so many, of course
but we need them sometimes
Give me a little more time
To catch up on the stories
or reflect on my youth.

I would use a little less sarcasm
Seems it has become a bit dry
Find a few more hangouts
The old ones became boring
Maybe even become bolder
Just a tad more
Enough to speak to the cute guys
Who ask for more than sex with a simple "Hi"
Maybe more masculinity

With Life, Of Love, & On Dying

What a nice big word.
For them, not me
Truth be told I need it to cope with reality
And to be reminded of mine and man's fault

Maybe we could use a bit more apathy
To balance out what society lost
Earn it
But not only from others
Maybe even reverence, but what do you know about that?
We will be seen AND heard
"I am real."
So you remember that

Take us away from the world
Remove me from the lies, hate, and deceit
With a hell lot more of
Me, me, me, mmmmmm
See how good it sounds
Now tell the world
How it feels
More of me and less of you

I Still Love You

I trusted you and you betrayed me
By breaking my heart like it didn't matter
Even when you lied I didn't care
You touched me but never really wanted it
You may have love me but you forgot to let me know
But I still love you

You held me in your arms only to push me away
You called and wouldn't speak
So then I called but with no answer
We both hurt me only you never really cared
Even I gave you me, only to be returned back void
I wanted you and you said you wanted me
Yet you were afraid to say it openly
We both tried but you didn't try hard enough
I defended you when you hated me
Then I forgave you and it didn't matter
Because I still love you

We shared, could've, and we even were for a moment
What a dream
We kissed and loved but not really
Please just tell me you love me
Because I still love you

The Cry of the Mistress

Relationships
Why don't they seem to last?
Cause you, he always moves around so fast
swaying them
playing them
Obviously persuading them
While I'm incessantly trying to poses him
Venture
on my adventure
try
fly
gliding side to side
Real High!
that is
On my love
I even open up a little
 To try and let you in
So you can choose to go back again
and again
to some other
Well ain't that a bitch?
Or is it me?

Maybe had I not called
You
Knowing how you'd feel
Momentarily
Often
For him or her, you know how you do
Over and over this truth we've been through
Yet still I wait

With Life, Of Love, & On Dying

Saving my love
Can't you see?
Cause that's just deep
Deep
Deep
I am weak
But you, baby you, you just don' know
Pain you never let heal
So let's hide it
I won't fight, ignore, or run from this
It's all my fault…

Maybe it would've worked
I say "Let's stay""
In my head are so many lies
But why oh why do I cry?
And sometimes somehow, I die
Only inside
That's just how it is sweet lost love
Why can't it be, a life
For just you, me, and she
Laughing, holding, yearning
For more loving
From another
Knowing you could never
Never ever give your life
To another, holding hands; loving a man.

Sure, I'll take all the blame
Even play your most dangerous game
Through all this sin, remorse, and shame
The mental, verbal, sometimes emotional abuse

fits of rage, hate, distrust, and deliberate misuse
Until you decide to claim
And give names
Better yet unable to obtain something more suitable for
you
What about the hearts you took
Not only mine
Following before and after

The Real

It seems as though I'm only trying to exist
Not living, or even seeking eternal bliss
Barely escaping the traps set by self
Agonizing and beautiful
I'm open to what it may bring
It seems to be what is true.
The Real.

We happen to long for a moment
Still in it we can't keep it or let it go
From breaking to only running
All for a sale of a glimpse
And to break means to love, truly
Learning more than phileo.
But of true agape. The Real.

Really... Really Not

Feelings of rejection and disgust
Faces portraying disinterest on becoming close
Close like vein and blood, pressing into the foreskin of
man
Pleasuring himself off of others
Torn and scarred by the words of his brothers
Left emotionless
Inattentive
Yet...

Knowingly we seem to forget
That we love. (Anyway)
That we are (Nothing)
And that we've become (Broken)
Shit guised as feelings
Showing no remorse
Of destroying virgin dreams
Of loving nameless dicks
Still loving?
Seemingly forever
Which only lasts minutes
Not hours
Minutes, lost in the fragmented mind
or seconds, of multiple orgasms from feeling inside
Simply overflowing with countless sex
The anticipation of "I Love You"
Really??

My Ken... Doll

My very first boy
Toy.

Baby, beautiful. My boo
No, it's just you.
I won't tell you I missed you
But we both know that I do
So let me tell you I love you
Then you can play with me too.
Time for show & tell, forget your old toys
Pay attention.
Now I want you to show me how you are, boy
Let's spin bottles
And make all kinds of noise
I can hide while you seek
Later sit at my table, I'll even serve you tea
Rather watch cartoons or whatever is on TV?
Lets' not play your game
You know that
One word, creep
Aww go to sleep
But Ken wants to freak
Oh how sweet
Now let me tell you how it feels
Still

Playmates, my first date
All that's left now but hate
Won't you say you are my heart
Because you are
And that's where it starts

With Life, Of Love, & On Dying

Inside
See baby my treasure you found it
Reassembled, rearranged
Banged and claimed
So very
Damn, hard!
Ahh.
I want to say why my heart beats
But I'm silicone and plastic right down to my feet
We were made together
All in one
But still parts, copies of you belong
Some
If only I worked without (batteries) won't you buy double
A
My secret in you- Made in China.
Feelings and love my face may express
Till you got shipped left, off towards the West
Fed Ex
UPS.
Wanting to free him
Ken that is
Then lines became thin
Now all Barbies come fully equipped
With their very own
Ken. Doll.

He Won't Teach Me How to Love Him (Anymore)

Of all the things I have learned
Heard, said, even whispered.
None of it.
Loud and brightly.
Or not.
Of all the things I wanted.
Including you I needed.
Yet above all these things
There is one thing I question.
So to you, lover, I propose.
A series of interviews and applications,
Questions beating the veins of my heart
(Thoughts even)
Additionally, some inquiring
Other distant minds.
So to my proposal again
Who would know?
If for a moment I gave
That part, island, waters surrounding
Of myself, to you
In return what would you do
How do I say those words
I look, as if your eyes hold forgiveness
Forgetfulness of this.
Is. Our business
How do I create a riddle
Sly enough
For your cunning
To show and inform
I must say this, lover
I must, lover

With Life, Of Love, & On Dying

Acceptance brings healing
Rejection hatred
It's not enough to say "Love me"
Not close when cries "I Love You"
And here again I digress from proposing
My life
To give you, knowingly
As if trying to love you
But for what purpose
It has been some long lonely times
Teaching me not how to love but how far I haven't loved
Farther than the stars
Indefinitely unlike reality
Yearning for one day holding
Won't you explain
Tell me
Write, sing, scream it
Paint it if you have to
Or mime if it works
Give me a sign so I may love you, fully and legally.
Teach me.
I propose again me to you
You.
The first real
Real real
Let's not dictate with classification
Damn it just teach me to love you

ON DYING

I'm dying to the World and the things it can't do 4 Me!
I'm sick of people lying for Fun and trying to discourage
me to the point of Suicide.
When u had it, u was walking round smelling yourself
and making fun of me and mines.
I need 2 learn this lesson quickly! I need 2 learn this lesson
quickly!
Its almost 2 years and I'm still chasing a Nightmare.
Losing my mind, abusing my health.
And for what a beautiful man, who has nothing else.
Continuously feeding on my spiritual wealth.
Nothing ever taught, learned, experienced, heard or
found out is ever just merely words
But a foreshadow of a series of decisions you will have to
make.

(Choices)
I'm so over you Nigga!
Well to be honest in a way I'm over myself too.
And I'm over all the rest of you!
I choose to love you because that's the only way I can be
free!
I choose to free you because I can't save you and it hurts!
I am hurting you because I need you to know you're not a
child anymore.
Let's just love each other knowingly without regret,
remorse or shame.
Let's love one another over again!

Again, over I say!
Again, until I fall over and Over again!

Newborn (In the Morning)

This irreversible scent of musk
Mixed with cologne and the stench of sex
Just hours before
Alcohol fills your nostrils
Stained sheets and drawn blinds
Room 320.
Beauty rises
A man of exotic commonness
Hold it.
Shower to wash the remains
Silk mingled with a stickiness
Wash
Rather, but should you repeat?
You ponder "Will this work?"
"What does he think?"
Thoughts flooding your mind
As the water temperature rises
The room is now empty
A note and number lie on the table
With 5 crisp $100 bills next to it
This month's rent
The night before occurs, constantly
The he comes and you cum
In your mind you make him yours
Beginning to want more than sex or money
And all things that reside in the in-between
You wonder what it'd be like
If maybe once he stayed, in the morning.

Frequently many lovers come and go
Leaving this bitter

Longing, lonely void
So, sleep. Step back
You remember when there was
One, two, preferably no more than three
A night
Hoping that against the odds
You'd find your type
The real Mr. Right
Yet they were all turned out
Running game
With breakfast at McDonald's
Degrading your worth
You wish to indulge
Commune with, share a little intellect with even
Maybe
Express, feel feelings
To talk
No.
False penetrations, deep thrusts, breakings in the soul
He acks depth with no knowledge
At least of another
See he'd rather the short long nights in you
In his arms
And oh, how strong those arms were
But I digress
Awakened from sleep
I cry and weep
"Do you really know me?"
In the literal, not biblical sense
"Do you know that I am more than just my body?"
"Do you know more than my head or how it feels?'
More than a slim figure

Or nice pretty lips
The kind that make men go wild
When you grab my waist what do you really see?
Is it the truth, a heart looking for love?
Or just someone to lay the dick to?
Yeah, that's what I thought
And I want more
I want to be loved in the morning

Local clubs
Becoming more and more the same
A damn meat market
To find you a piece of
To shoot
Then release
Lies, lines, niggas.
Yet they seem to excite
Someone who's had all the girls
The girls both unknown and well known as "sissies"
But to you he's hot
A.K.A. Mr. Hot Boy B.K.A Mr. Good Dick
What the fuck?
He smashes, what seems to be the life out of you
Breaking your back from the beginnings of Genesis to the
end of Revelation
But who cares the shit feels good
S E X!
Now you done went and lost your friends
Cause they all had him in the morning.

Now maybe you have heard of me
The local hoe/celebrity

I go around fulfilling fantasies
Orgasm among countless orgasm
Mixed with the risk of popular STDs, revealing the true
story
In anger he gives back
Destroying homes, families, and lives
Yeah well isn't he sexy?
They wanted him.
Until the drug affects start to complicate already bad
living habits
Now he preys on the young
The young, dumb, and full of cum
While I taught him tricks and he trained em like babies
Cause they would never think twice
Bout the broke condoms and swallowed semen
From the past
But one day they will wake up
Like I did
When I ran away from home
And decided to have sex in the morning.

Poison in My Soul

This sickness supersedes.
Trying to control all of my
  Needs
   my being
  dreams and beliefs
From wanting and fervently longing, for another
To hold or cling on to
Let inside
Introduce to this deadly and powerful thing
That stops me from loving
    and sharing
What's deep.... much deeper
Than the true color of my days
It cuts me inside
Piercing more than any blade
Could it be God's gift
Although it appears man-made
Keeping men, women, even youth (lovers)
From each other
Lively diseases
Viruses non and communicable
Spreading
Across the body of man
Coursing through the entire
Of loveless souls
Who are still searching not knowing
that their desires for forbidden passion
Is serious
Yes as serious as every last orgasm
Abandoned and hopeless
This grieving taboo still passes

Only because of unforgotten agony
From being ripped and stolen on the inside
Causing bodies to twist and cry out
Only for love

NF (Non-Immediate Family)
(For The Family With Living Without)
We all said I love you
But I hate who you are
your ego
 even the way you talk
it all makes no sense
to be in love with....
Someone
who I'd rather see dead
God knows
I can't understand
how you think
    how you see
        feel perfect
Deadly ain't ya.
Enticing, intriguing, ignorant.
but you just
    so
      Fucking Stupid.

Muses

I see
And do you know what I see?
As you notice and watch
Soon, you see
That I see
You
The Whole
Home of the complexities
Or broken lies
But of what you really are
Pages like the sands
That Joshua
Or the Yeshua
Wrote on
When He Himself,
First
Saw, you.

Change

Chill winds that blow
While bathing in this sensual afterglow
You knowing in your mind
Expressing exploitation
Of the holding and molding
men showing and growing, into
Nothing
Into
Bliss burned down tired scenes
Letting go and going with the flow
until it screams
And becomes
Hopeless, like overflowing running water
Searching
While you remain thirsty
From the soul's evil promotions
Unrelenting and reproaching
Becoming freer like oceans
Perceiving every moment
With unknown useless focus
Using the lies
To accommodate the life
Learning lessons
With the worst of your own blessings
Neglected and unchosen
Hoping and believing to be perceived as a hope someone
one day can achieve.

www.ingramcontent.com/pod-product-compliance
Lightning Source LLC
Chambersburg PA
CBHW060042050426
42448CB00012B/3111